The Very Best of

RECURRING DREAM

Folio © 1996 International Music Publications Ltd
Southend Road, Woodford Green, Essex IG8 8HN

Worldwide Representation Grant Thomas Management

Music Transcribed by Barnes Music Engraving Ltd., East Sussex TN22 4HA
Printed by The Panda Group · Haverhill · Suffolk CB9 8PR · UK
Binding by ABS · Cambridge

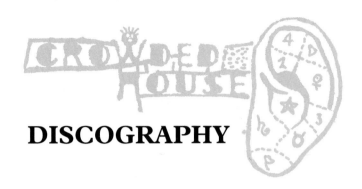

DISCOGRAPHY

Line-Up
NEIL FINN - songwriter\vocals\guitars
NICK SEYMOUR - bass\vocals
MARK HART - guitars\keyboards

Brief History
Crowded House emerged from the ashes of Split Enz, who split up in 1984. The band formed in Melbourne, Australia 1985 by ex-Split Enz members Neil Finn, drummer Paul Hester and bassist Nick Seymour.

1986 - Signed to Capitol Records and moved to L.A. to work with producer Mitchell Froom on their eponymous debut album.

1988 - Crowded House return to Australia.

1990 - Tim Finn (ex-Split Enz) and Neil write 'WOODFACE' album.

1991 - Tim joins band for world tour and departs Autumn '91. He is replaced by US session man Mark Hart.

1992 - Youth produces 'TOGETHER ALONE'. It is recorded at Kare Kare Beach in Auckland, New Zealand. All previous albums were recorded in L.A.

1994 - Drummer Paul Hester leaves.

1996 - Crowded House record three new tracks, "Instinct," "Not The Girl You Think You Are" and "Everything Is Good For You" to feature on 'RECURRING DREAM, The Very Best of CROWDED HOUSE'.

UK Releases

SINGLES

August	'86	WORLD WHERE YOU LIVE
April	'87	DON'T DREAM IT'S OVER
August	'87	SOMETHING SO STRONG
June	'88	BETTER BE HOME SOON
August	'88	SISTER MADLY
June	'91	CHOCOLATE CAKE
October	'91	FALL AT YOUR FEET
February	'92	WEATHER WITH YOU
June	'92	FOUR SEASONS IN ONE DAY
September	'92	IT'S ONLY NATURAL
September	'93	DISTANT SUN
November	'93	NAILS IN MY FEET
February	'94	LOCKED OUT
May	'94	FINGERS OF LOVE
September	'94	PINEAPPLE HEAD
June	'96	INSTINCT
August	'96	NOT THE GIRL YOU THINK YOU ARE

ALBUMS

September	'86	CROWDED HOUSE
July	'88	TEMPLE OF LOW MEN
July	'91	WOODFACE
October	'93	TOGETHER ALONE
June	'96	RECURRING DREAM, The Very Best of CROWDED HOUSE

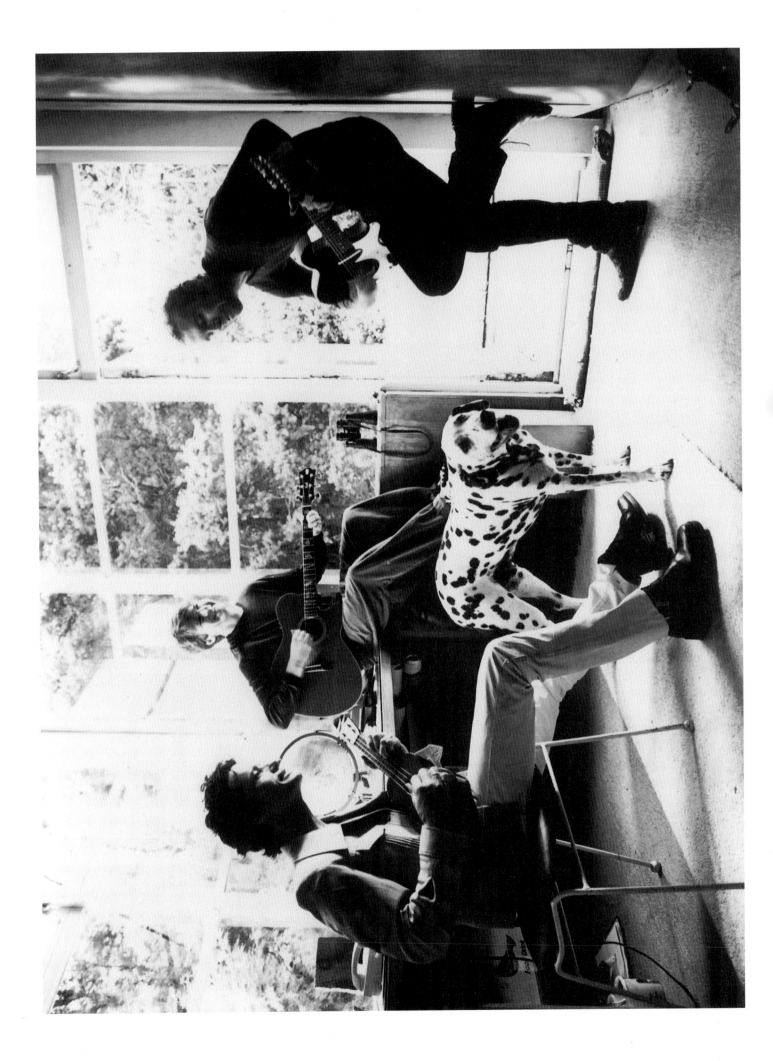

The Very Best of

RECURRING DREAM

Over the next few months you might hear a lot of Crowded House. Some songs you'll remember intimately - after all, 'Don't Dream its Over' and 'Weather With You' have passed into folk memory. That's expected. It'll be the others though, that catch you off guard. The way 'Four Seasons In One Day' injects fresh foreboding into the air like an oncoming storm; the unmistakable way that 'Distant Sun' has of identifying itself with a chorus you could gladly mistake for an old friend. It's the thing that Crowded House do best - slipping beneath your skin bearing all the hallmarks of Great Pop, so that before you can find out if the symptoms are normal, your mind's already made up. Crowded House, you see, are the nearest you'll get to a musical truth drug.

So, that seems like one good reason to put out a concise resume of Neil Finn's songs. Another reason for the release of 'Recurring Dream' lies in the fact that Crowded House have been together for 10 years. When Neil Finn and drummer Paul Hester dusted themselves down from the ashes of Split Enz, and welcomed Nick Seymour (bass/rollerblades) into the fold, there was no masterplan, just a desire to write some cool tunes very quickly and try them out on new audiences. Setting a trend that gathered apace for the next decade, new audiences responded with a zeal that suggested some kind of listener/band chemistry was afoot. Among those first songs were included 'When You Come' and the exultant embrace of 'Something So Strong' - both included here.

Another song present on those initial sessions was 'Don't Dream It's Over'. Within a year of its creation, it became Crowded House's first worldwide hit. Certain people were, surprised - bands don't usually get to Number Two in America by writing abstract ballads about such simple emotions. But then, Crowded House and the rule book have never seen eye to eye, finding new ways to fuse rapture and regret with every new album. 'Weather With You' - another global success from the platinum-selling 'Woodface' makes for the unlikeliest of hit singles with its muted rhythmic shuffle and impromptu meditations about Julius Caesar. But that's the thing about Crowded House. You never wonder why. Because you only look for reasons when something isn't working.

If you haven't seen Crowded House in concert, then have a listen to the second CD on 'Recurring Dream', which collects some of Crowded House's most memorable live appearances - improvised and otherwise. However, if you have seen them live, you certainly won't need prompting - you'll already know there's no group in the world like Crowded House, no Crowded House gig like the one you saw tonight. Whereas so many bands seem to fight against the spontaneity of a live situation in order to live up to their recorded work, Crowded House seem to thrive on it. For every moment of forlorn grace, there's always something just around the corner to keep you on your toes - be it the London gig when one fan, hardly able to contain himself, jumped on stage and stripped off; or that time the boys were so surprised by the volume of demand for their fourth encore that they ambled back on stage in their dressing gowns. If Crowded House's music reflects the wonderful cultural confusion of an Irish Catholic upbringing carried out in a New Zealand country town, the feeling Neil Finn's songs leave us with is much simpler. Even when playing those huge arenas so ill-equipped for intimacy, Crowded House have never had trouble turning events into the kind of family get-togethers you had as a kid. And while band members have come and gone (Neil's brother Tim briefly joined for 'Woodface', 'mysterious' guitarist Mark Hart joined for 'Together Alone', and Paul Hester left in 1994) the ambience has remained unchanged: 'That's the only way we know how to do it', said Neil in 1988, 'We're really flying on the seat of our pants whenever we play live, and I think the audience knows that. That's where the buzz comes in.'

Welcome to the songs of Crowded House...

Weather With You

Words and Music by
Neil Finn and Tim Finn

Verse 2:
Well, there's a small boat made of china
It's going nowhere on the mantelpiece
Well, do I lie like a lounge room lizard
Or do I sing like a bird released?

World Where You Live

Words and Music by
Neil Finn

Medium

Here's some-one now____ whose got the mus - cle.
So here we lie____ a - gainst each oth - er.

His stead - y hand____ could move a moun-tain. Ex - pert in bed,____
These four walls____ can nev - er hold us. We're look-ing for____

but come on now, there must be some-thing miss - ing.____
wide o - pen spac - es high a - bove the kitch - en.____

Fall At Your Feet

Words and Music by
Neil Finn

1. I'm real-ly close to-night

and I feel_ like I'm mov-ing in-side_ her,
there's some-thing in_ the way_ that you're talk-ing,

ly-ing in_ the dark_____
words don't sound_ right,

and I think that I'm_ be-gin
but I hear them_ all

Locked Out

Words and Music by
Neil Finn

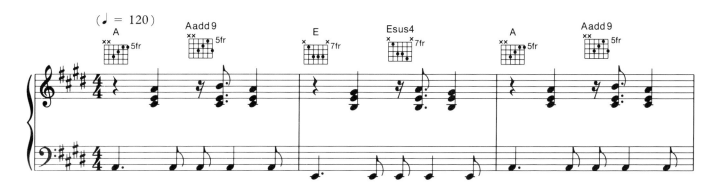

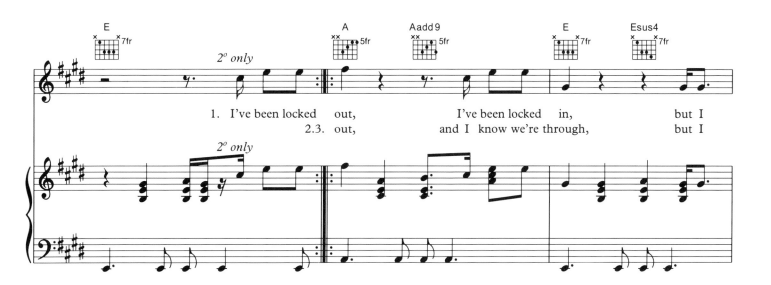

1. I've been locked   out,   I've been locked   in,   but I
2.3.   out,   and I know we're through,   but I

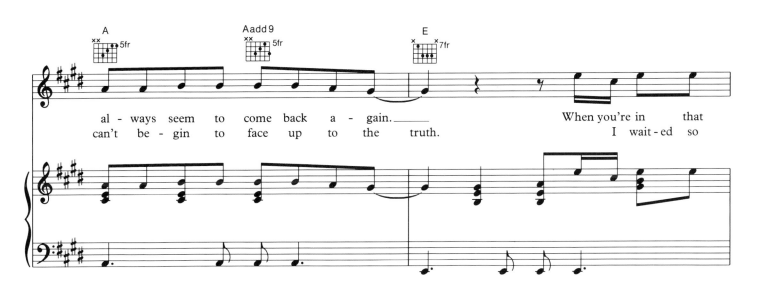

al - ways seem to   come back a - gain._____   When you're in   that
can't be - gin to   face up to the   truth.   I wait - ed so

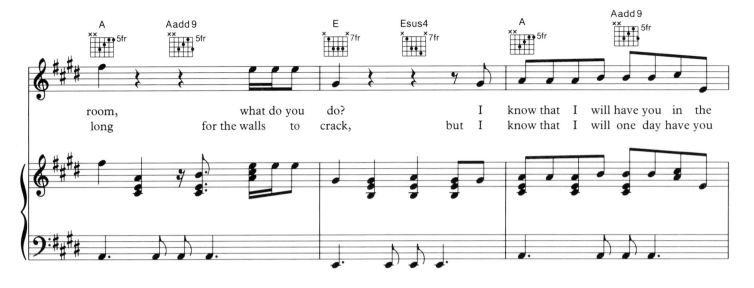

room, what do you do? I know that I will have you in the
long for the walls to crack, but I know that I will one day have you

end. And the clouds,___ they are cry-ing on you, and the
back. And the hills___ are as soft as a pil-low, and they
And I work with the bees and the hon-ey, and

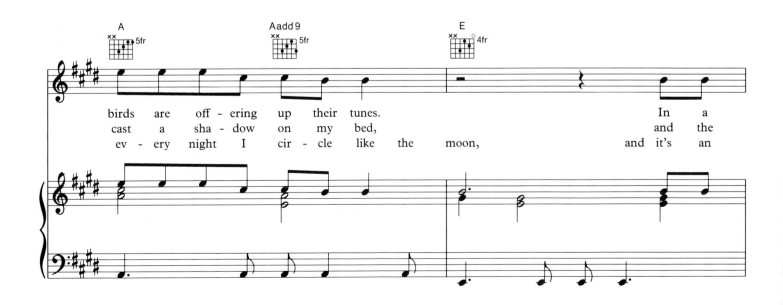

birds are off-er-ing up their tunes. In a
cast a sha-dow on my bed, and the
ev-ery night I cir-cle like the moon, and it's an

28

Don't Dream It's Over

Words and Music by
Neil Finn

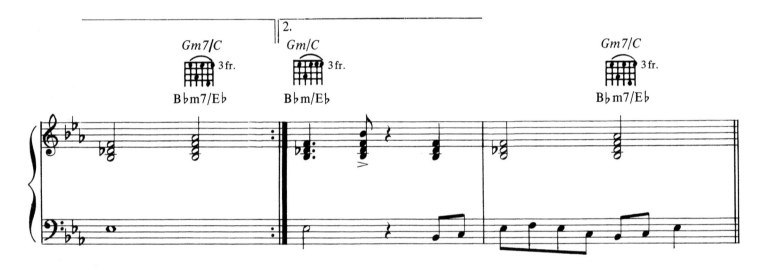

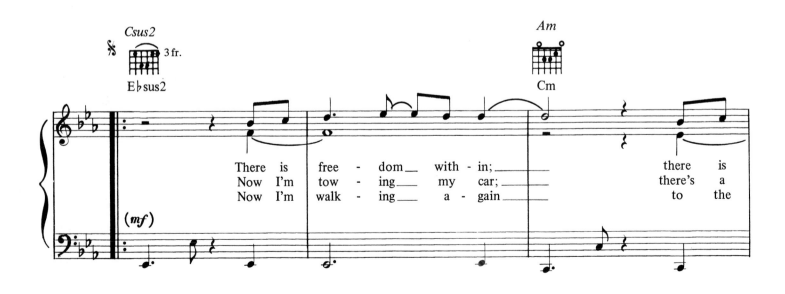

There is free - dom__ with - in;__ there is
Now I'm tow - ing__ my car;__ there's a
Now I'm walk - ing__ a - gain to the

* Pianists: Omit lead vocal melody till end.

Into Temptation

Words and Music by
Neil Finn

42

Pineapple Head

Words and Music by
Neil Finn

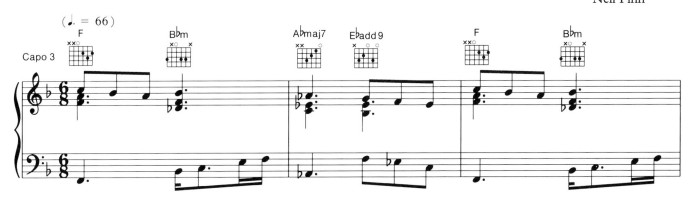

1. De - tec - tive is flat, no long - er is
(2.) lu - cid as hell, and these i - ma - ges

al - ways flat out, got the num - ber of the get - a - way car,
mov - ing so fast, like a fe - ver so close to the bone, I

did - n't get ve - ry far.
don't feel____ too well.

2. As

And if____ you choose to take____ that

path, I will play you like a shark,____ and I'll

clutch at your heart, I'll come fly - ing like a spark__

path, would you come to make me

pay? I will play you like a shark, and I'll

When You Come

Words and Music by
Neil Finn

Private Universe

Words and Music by
Neil Finn

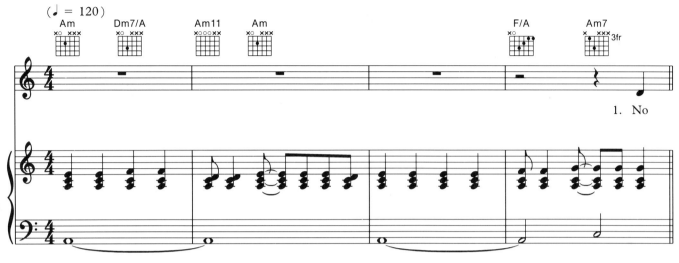

1. No

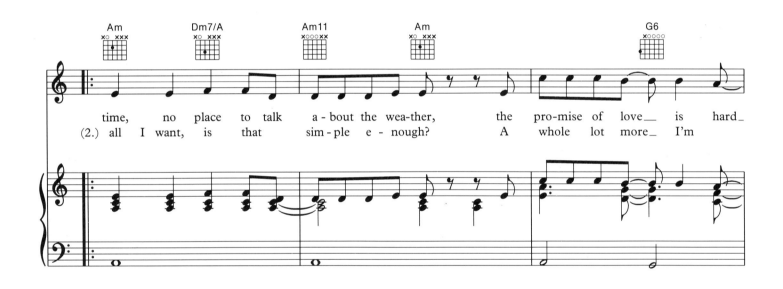

time, no place to talk a-bout the wea-ther, the pro-mise of love___ is hard___
(2.) all I want, is that sim-ple e-nough? A whole lot more___ I'm

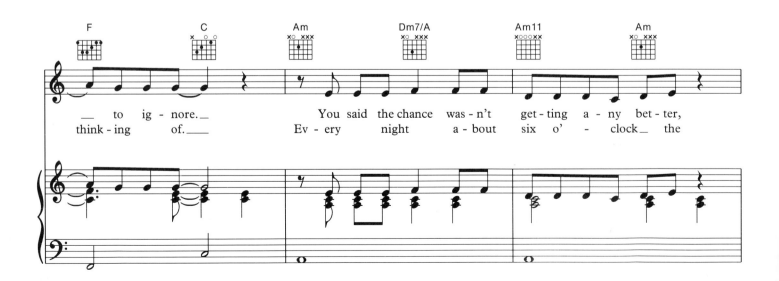

___ to ig - nore.___ You said the chance was-n't get-ting a - ny bet-ter,
think-ing of.___ Ev-ery night a-bout six o'-clock___ the

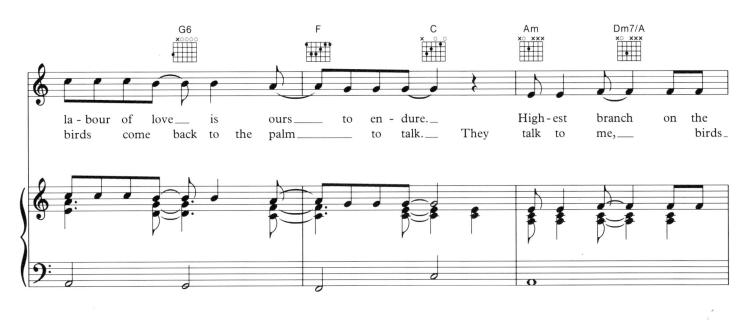

la - bour of love___ is ours___ to en - dure.___ High - est branch on the
birds come back to the palm_____ to talk.___ They talk to me,___ birds_

ap - ple tree,___ it was my fav - ourite place___ to be.___
___ talk to me, if I go___ down on_____ my knees.___

1st time only

I could hear__ them break-ing free,__ but they could not see__ me.__

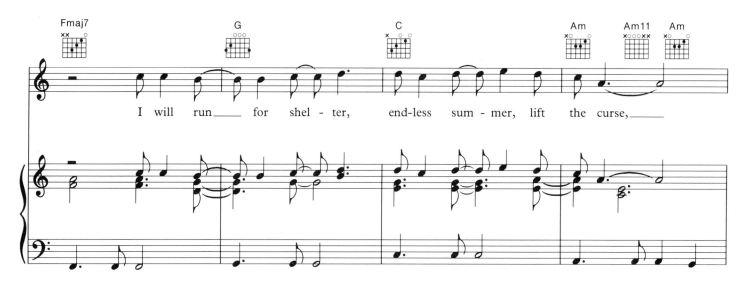

I will run___ for shel - ter, end-less sum - mer, lift the curse,___

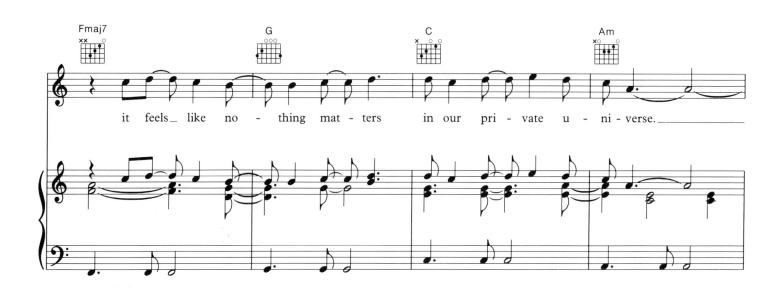

it feels_ like no - thing mat - ters in our pri - vate u - ni - verse.___

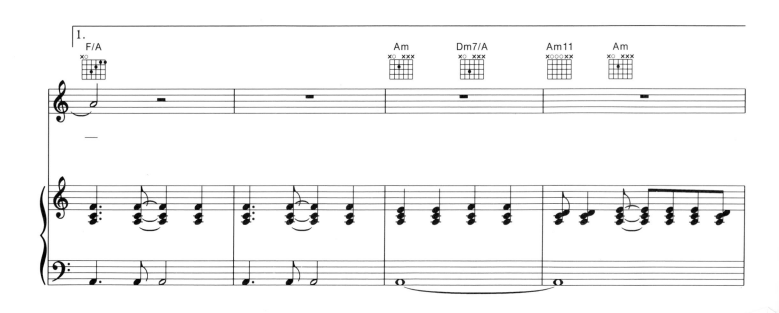

and it's a plea-sure that I have known,_____ oh._____

It's a tight squeeze, but I won't let go.__

Not The Girl
You Think You Are

Words and Music by
Neil Finn

You're not the girl you think you are, no, no.

They're not his shoes un-der your bed,___ yeah.___

He'll take you pla-ces in his car___ that you won't for-get,___

no._____ Ah,_____

Instinct

Words and Music by
Neil Finn

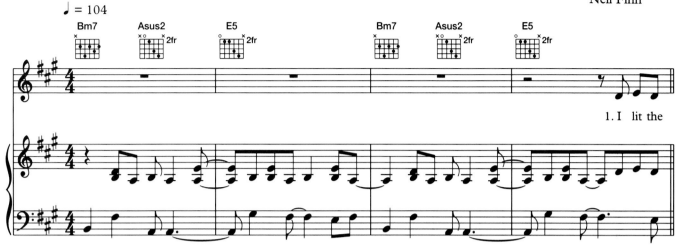

1. I lit the

match,   I lit the match,   I saw an - oth - er mon - ster turn to ash,   felt the
(2.) fic - tion   from the fact___   I been a lit - tle slow to re - act___   but it's

bur - den lift - ing from my back.___   Do you re - cog - nize the ner - vous twitch_   that ex - pos -
near - ly time to flick the switch_   and I'm hang - ing by a sin - gle stitch_   laugh - ing

I Feel Possessed

Words and Music by
Neil Finn

Four Seasons In One Day

Words and Music by
Neil Finn and Tim Finn

1. Four seasons in one day lying in the depths of your imagination,
2. Smiling as the shit comes down, you can tell a man from what he has to say.

worlds above and worlds below, the sun shines on the black clouds hanging over the domain.
Everything gets turned around and I will risk my neck again, again remain.

Even when you're feeling warm, the
you can take me where you will

It's Only Natural

Words and Music by
Neil Finn and Tim Finn

repeat to fade

Distant Sun

Words and Music by
Neil Finn

1. Tell me all the things you would change,
(2.) still so young to tra-vel so far,

I don't pre-tend to know what you want,
old e-nough to know who you are,

when you

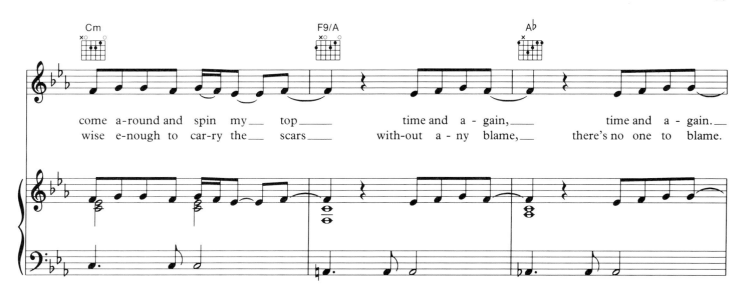

come a-round and spin my___ top_____ time and a - gain,_____ time and a - gain.___
wise e-nough to car-ry the__ scars____ with-out a - ny blame,____ there's no one to blame.

__ No fire_____ where I lit my spark,___
__ It's ea - sy to for - get what you learned,__

I am not a-fraid of the dark,_____ where your words de-vour__ my heart,
wait-ing for the thrill to re - turn,___ feel - ing your de - sire_____ burn,_

ven-geance from a - bove,_____ I don't pre-tend to know what you want,_____ but I off - er love.

Se - ven worlds will col - lide_____ when -

Something So Strong

Words and Music by
Neil Finn and Mitchell Froom

Mean To Me

Words and Music by
Neil Finn

Better Be Home Soon

Words and Music by
Neil Finn

102

D.S. al Coda

Coda

soon. _____ Oh. _____ That's why I tell ____ you,

Freely

Tacet

you'd bet - ter be home ____ soon.

molto rit.

p

Everything Is Good For You

Words and Music by
Neil Finn

I see a man with a flag___ and he leads_ the pro-cess - ion

see a wo-man shed-ding tears___ for a man_ locked in pri -

Ev-ery-thing is good for you,   if   it does-n't kill you.

Ev-ery-thing is good for you,   if   it does-n't kill   you._____

Ev-ery-thing is good for you, it's good for you.

play 4 times

repeat to fade

Exclusive Distributors

International Music Publications Limited
Southend Road, Woodford Green, Essex IG8 8HN, England

International Music Publications Limited
25 Rue D'Hautville, 75010 Paris, France

International Music Publications GmbH, Germany
Marstallstraße 8, D-80539 Munchen, Germany

Nuova Carish S.R.L.
Via M.F. Quintiliano 40, 20138 Milano, Italy

Danmusik
Vognmagergade 7, DK-1120 Copenhagen K, Denmark

Warner Bros Publications Inc
15800 NW 48th Avenue, Miami, Florida 33014, USA

Warner/Chappell Music Inc, Australia
1 Cassins Avenue, North Sydney, New South Wales 2060, Australia

Printed in England
The Panda Group · Haverhill · Suffolk · 1/97

OTHER CROWDED HOUSE TITLES PUBLISHED BY
IMP

CROWDED HOUSE

Piano · Vocal · Guitar

Order Ref. 14520

TEMPLE OF LOW MEN

Piano · Vocal · Guitar

Order Ref. 14521

WOODFACE

Piano · Vocal · Guitar

Order Ref. 18705

TOGETHER ALONE

Piano · Vocal · Guitar

Order Ref. 2093A

AVAILABLE FROM ALL GOOD MUSIC STORES

For a free catalogue of IMP titles, please write to the address below
stating your areas of interest:
International Music Publications Limited
Southend Road, Woodford Green, Essex IG8 8HN, England.